Elijah McCoy | Inventor

Written by Garnet Nelson Jackson
Illustrated by Gary Thomas

MODERN CUR̶̶̶̶̶̶̶̶̶̶̶ ̶ ̶ ̶̶̶̶̶RESS

Program Reviewers

Maureen Besst, Teacher
   Orange County Public Schools
   Orlando, Florida

Carol Brown, Director of Reading
   Freeport Schools
   Freeport, New York

Kanani Choy, Principal
   Clarendon Alternative School
   San Francisco, California

Barbara Jackson-Nash, Deputy Director
   Banneker-Douglass Museum
   Annapolis, Maryland

Minesa Taylor, Teacher
   Mayfair Elementary School
   East Cleveland, Ohio

MODERN CURRICULUM PRESS
13900 Prospect Road, Cleveland, Ohio 44136

Simon & Schuster • A Paramount Communications Company

Copyright © 1993 Modern Curriculum Press, Inc.

Library of Congress Cataloging-in-Publication Data

Jackson, Garnet
   Elijah McCoy, inventor/written by Garnet Nelson Jackson; illustrated by Gary Thomas.
      p. cm.
   Summary: A simple biography of an African American engineer who invented the automatic lubricator for railway systems and thus gave rise to the phrase "the real McCoy."
   1. McCoy, Elijah, 1844-1929 — Juvenile literature. 2. African American inventors — United States — Biography — Juvenile literature. 3. Lubricating systems — Biography — Juvenile literature. [1. McCoy, Elijah, 1844-1929. 2. Inventors. 3. African Americans — Biography.]
I. Thomas, Gary, 1936-   ill. II. Title.
T40.M43J33   1933   609.2 — dc20   [B]   92-28797   CIP   AC
ISBN 0-8136-5230-8: (Reinforced Binding)   ISBN 0-8136-5703-2: (Paperback)

Text Printed on Recycled Paper

Swish Swissh Swisssh Swissssssh!
The train wheels came to a halt.
It was oiling time again.

1

A little over 100 years ago, trains did not move as fast as they do today.

A train would run a while before the engine slowed to a stop. Then workers would have to oil every moving part before the train could start again.

It would take days and days, sometimes weeks, before cargo was delivered. Sometimes goods would spoil or rot on the way.

3

There lived in a little Canadian town called
Colchester, Ontario, a small boy named
Elijah McCoy. Like most children, he liked
trains. He loved watching the trains near his
home and listening to the *swish swish*
sounds of the big wheels.

But he did not know how hard it was to keep those big wheels turning. He did not know that, if they were not stopped and oiled many times, the wheels would be unable to move.

6

Elijah was the McCoys' greatest joy.
His parents, Mildred and George,
had been runaway slaves from
Kentucky who fled the United States
to Canada.

They took great pride in their young
son. George worked many long
hours to make sure Elijah had a
good education.

Some time later the family moved
to Ypsilanti, Michigan. Elijah spent
much of his spare time trying to
design and improve machines.

Before he finished school, he left
for Scotland. There Elijah studied to
become a mechanical engineer.

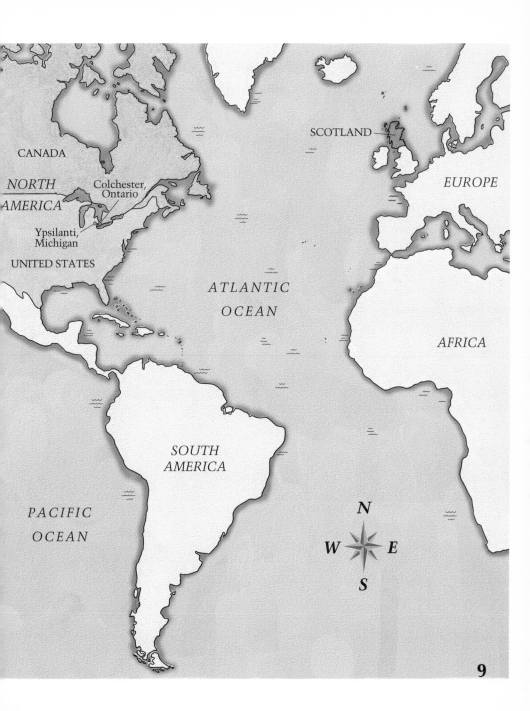

CANADA

NORTH
AMERICA

Colchester,
Ontario

Ypsilanti,
Michigan

UNITED STATES

SCOTLAND

EUROPE

ATLANTIC
OCEAN

AFRICA

SOUTH
AMERICA

PACIFIC
OCEAN

N
W ✦ *E*
S

Elijah learned to be a great engineer. Then he returned to the United States in search of a job.

But because of his color, Elijah could not find a job as an engineer. So he settled for a job as an oiler for trains. This was quite a lowly job for the fine engineer he was.

As Elijah oiled the wheels, he
remembered the *swish swish*
sounds of the wheels he loved as
a boy.

Now he knew how hard it was to
keep them moving, and how
long it took a train to get from
place to place.

Elijah thought, "There must be some way that a train can be oiled while moving."

That way it would never have to
stop. And the wheels would continue
to go *swish swish.*

After much thinking, in 1872 Elijah McCoy made a new part for trains. This part dripped oil onto the moving wheels and the engine while the train was rolling along the tracks. Elijah called his new part a *lubricator.*

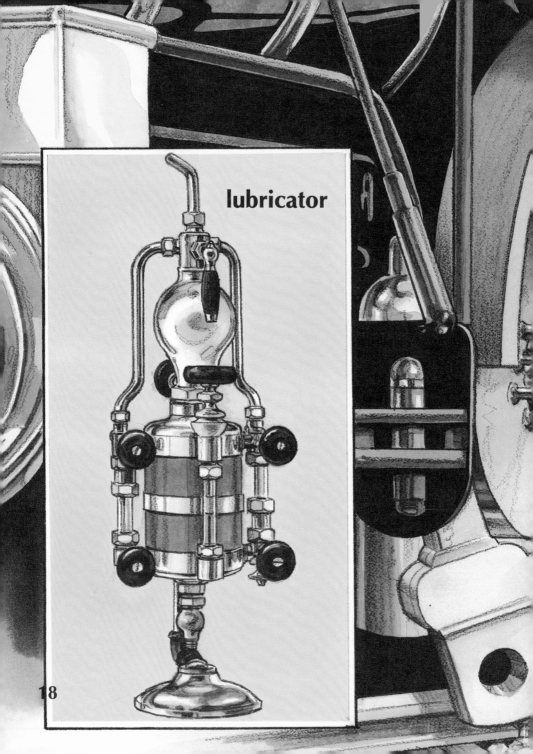

lubricator

18

News about the lubricator
spread. Railroad people
everywhere were happy.
Trains no longer had to stop
to be oiled.

Elijah invented lubricators for other machines, too. People in businesses all over the world were buying Elijah McCoy's lubricators.

Since everyone wanted to buy lubricators, other people tried to make and sell them. But theirs just did not work as well as Elijah's.

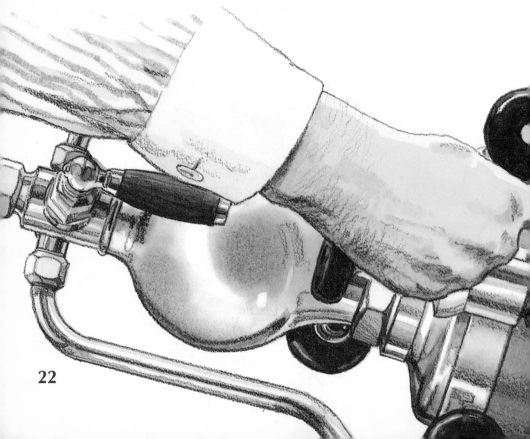

Merchants wanted to make sure they were not getting a copy. So when they went to buy a lubricator, they always asked for "the real McCoy."

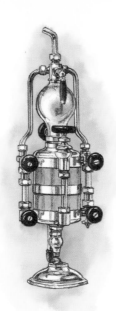

Elijah became famous and wealthy as one of the greatest mechanical engineers of his time.

And from that day, our world has never been the same. McCoy's ideas are still used in lubricators for cars, trains, planes, and many other machines. And the saying "the real McCoy" is still used to describe "the very best."

Glossary

engineer (en jə nir´) 1. A person who runs an engine, such as a railroad locomotive. 2. A person who plans and builds engines and other machines, roads, bridges, and buildings.

lubricator (loo´ bri kāt ər) Something that adds oil or other material to a thing to make it smooth

machine (mə shēn´) Anything that is made of one or more parts, often moving parts, to do work

mechanical engineer (mə kan´ i k'l en jə nir´) An engineer who plans and builds new machines or makes machines run better

merchant (mʉr´ chənt) A person, such as a store owner, who makes a living by buying and selling

slave (slāv) A person who is owned by someone else, and must do whatever the owner wants